THE WORLD HERITAGE

PRE-COLUMBIAN PEOPLES OF NORTH AMERICA

CHILDRENS PRESS®

CHICAGO

Table of Contents

Library of Congress Cataloging-in-Publication Data
Cordoba, Maria.
  [Tribus precolombinas de Norteamerica. English]
  Pre-Columbian Peoples of North America / by Maria Cordoba.
    p. cm. — (The World heritage)
  Includes index.
  ISBN 0-516-08393-7
  1. Indians of North America—Antiquities—Juvenile literature. 2. Indians of
North America—History—Juvenile literature. [1. Indians of North America—
History.] I. Title. II. Series.
E71.C7813   1994
970.01—dc20   94-16112
                                                          CIP
                                                           AC

Pre-Columbian Peoples of North America

From about 200,000 to about 15,000 years ago, during the Pleistocene Era, glaciers formed throughout the earth. As these glaciers grew, the sea level dropped. The Bering and Chukchi Seas separated, creating a land bridge between present-day Siberia and Alaska. People and animals could freely cross it from Asia into the Americas. These immigrants belonged to our own species, known as Homo sapiens. They knew how to make such tools as spear points and axes. These nomadic people gathered wild plants and hunted bison and mammoths. Over thousands of years, they adapted to the diverse regions of the new American continent, giving rise to a variety of tribes, languages, and cultures.

The City with the Astronomical Observatory
At Cahokia Mounds lived one of North America's most important pre-Columbian cultures, known as the Mississippian culture. More than 120 mounds were originally built at this site. It is located in southern Illinois near the confluence of the Missouri and Mississippi rivers. Fewer than forty-five of these mounds still exist. The lower photo shows the main mound, Monk's Mound. Upon it was built the principal temple or the residence of the political and religious leader. In the top photo is what is known as the "American Woodhenge." The Indians used it to measure the changing seasons. Cahokia had a highly precise astronomical monument.

4

Pre-Columbian Civilizations

At the time Christopher Columbus arrived, about forty million native people lived in the Americas. The continent embraced a wide range of cultures—from hunting and gathering societies and small farming communities to powerful empires. But the arrival of Europeans led to a major decline in population. There were many reasons for this decline: epidemics of smallpox, measles, typhus, and influenza; starvation; and the violence of the conquest. The Amerindians had little hope for survival. Many civilizations disappeared, leaving little but a memory. Fortunately, however, many people and many cultures survived and live throughout the Americas today.

Life in the Arctic: The Eskimos

The Eskimos live in the northernmost region of North America, from Alaska to Greenland. Probably the Eskimos were the wave of immigrants who had lived in Siberia and came across the Bering Strait. They are a people who live upon the resources of the sea, such as whales, seals, and fish.

Vikings in the New World
At the northernmost point of Newfoundland was a Norse settlement known as L'Anse aux Meadows. It proves that the Vikings arrived in the New World long before Columbus. The eight buildings discovered there were used as dwellings or workshops. The photo at the right shows the archaeological remains of one of these workshops. The photo above shows one of the many bays of northern Newfoundland.

The direct ancestors of today's Eskimos, or Inuit, were the Thule. By A.D. 1100, the Thule inhabited all of northern Canada and Greenland. They were the first American natives who came into contact with the Norsemen when they arrived in the New World.

The people of the Thule culture lived in round houses that were built partly underground. With bone, wood, and stone, they made weapons for hunting and fishing. Some of their weapons that have been found include harpoons, knives, spears, and darts. They hunted and traveled in one-person boats called kayaks and larger boats called umiaks. Both were made of seal skin stretched over a wood frame.

Like the Eskimos today, the Thule people were able to adapt magnificently to a hostile environment with scarce resources. They even made decorative objects. Archaeologists have found some of their unique artistic creations made out of ivory, bone, and wood.

The Forest Dwellers

Canada's vast forests and tundra were inhabited by nomadic hunters who lived in seasonal camps, following the caribou herds. For them, the caribou provided not only meat, but also hides for clothing and bone for tools and utensils.

Many of the groups that inhabited this region disappeared in the first centuries A.D., due to the harsh climate and the limited resources. But when Europeans reached the New World, the sub-Arctic region was completely settled with native people. They spoke the Athabaskan and Algonquian languages.

The Totem as Symbol
On Anthony Island, in the Queen Charlotte Archipelago off the coast of British Columbia, the ancestors of the Haida Indians lived for some two thousand years. At many sites along the northwest coast of Canada and the west coast of Alaska are remnants of abandoned nineteenth-century villages such as Ninstints (opposite page). There several totem poles still stand, made of western red cedar. Each pole represented a clan. They were decorated with the images of creatures well-known to the tribe: ravens, bears, wolves, eagles, and so on. The map shows locations in the United States and Canada that UNESCO has declared World Heritage sites because they preserve pre-Columbian remains.

Pre-Columbian Timeline

c. 15,000 years ago—*Homo sapiens* reached the American continent.

9th century A.D.—The Vikings settled in Iceland and Greenland.

c. A.D. 1001—Leif Eriksson sailed to Newfoundland and named it Vinland.

1492—Christopher Columbus landed in the New World.

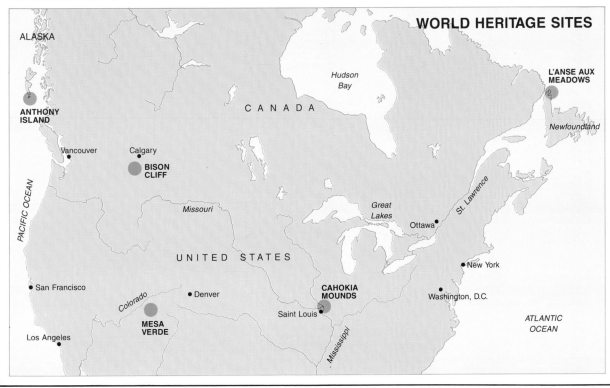

ALASKA

Hudson
Bay

C A N A D A

L'ANSE AUX
MEADOWS

ANTHONY
ISLAND

Newfoundland

Vancouver

Calgary

BISON
CLIFF

PACIFIC OCEAN

Missouri

Great
Lakes

St. Lawrence

Ottawa

UNITED STATES

New York

San Francisco

Denver

CAHOKIA
MOUNDS

Colorado

Washington, D.C.

Saint Louis

ATLANTIC
OCEAN

MESA
VERDE

Los Angeles

Mississippi

Like the Eskimos, the people of the sub-Arctic adapted to the cold Canadian climate. During the long winters, they survived by fishing with the fishing nets they fashioned. The Athabaskans devised a type of snowshoe, which they tied to their feet in order to travel over the snow. They spent the spring and summer hunting game and fishing from canoes. They stored food for the winter. The Algonquians gathered wild rice on the swampy shallows of lakes.

The most common type of dwelling in the region was a dome-shaped hut called the *wigwam* in the Algonquian language. This was a cone-shaped tent of posts covered with skins or bark.

The Fishermen of the Northwest

On the northwestern coast, on a narrow strip of land between the Canadian Rocky Mountains and the Pacific Ocean, lived numerous independent culture groups. The Haida and the Tlingit stand out among them for their political and social organization. Along this steep coast, cut by hundreds of fjords and islands, the canoe was the chief means of communication and transportation.

Fish was the region's main resource. Hunting was important during seasons when the fish grew scarce. The people's most important building material was wood. Besides their dwellings, they made wooden totem poles, canoes, bowls, spoons, masks, and other objects. All were finely worked with artistic motifs.

The Farmers of the Southwest

The so-called "desert cultures" were adapted to the dry climate of southwestern North America. Some two thousand years ago, these people gave up their nomadic life and became sedentary. As farmers, they cultivated corn, beans, and squash.

The Hohokam, who lived in the desert that is now in southern Arizona, built great stone and adobe houses. For their temples, they built flat-topped pyramids. The Mogollon lived in Arizona and New Mexico, in small villages of semi-underground houses. Best-known were the Anasazi, ancestors of the present-day Pueblo Indians.

The Houses of the Cliff Dwellers
Some 1,300 years ago, the Anasazi Indians settled in Mesa Verde, located in southwestern Colorado. The Anasazi were among the best-known and most highly developed cultures of North America. Typical of this culture are buildings carved out of steep cliffs. These were massive, apartment-like dwellings. The photos show three views of Mesa Verde National Park.

10

The first people who settled this territory earned the name Basketmakers due to their great skill at making utensils with esparto, a type of grass. The Basketmakers built semi-underground houses. They lived by a combination of hunting, gathering, and farming.

The descendants of Basketmakers began to make elevated houses of wood and clay, with connected rooms. Underground, they built kivas—circular structures used for religious ceremonies. They built their homes around the kiva. The clay walls helped cool the rooms so they could endure the region's extreme climate.

In the eleventh century, or Classic Period, the Anasazi reached the height of their development. Around the kivas they built multi-storied stone dwellings, much like apartment houses. For unknown reasons, the civilization began to decline in the twelfth century. Some evidence suggests that a multi-year drought may have been the cause.

The Peoples of the Plains

Between the Mississippi River and the Rocky Mountains stretched a vast prairie called the Great Plains. Here lived the Sioux, Caddo, Blackfeet, Kiowa, and other Indian groups. They were the genuine models for the horse-mounted warriors of the movie screen.

Circular Temples
One of the most important constructions of Mesa Verde is Balcony House. It consists of a great patio with a vaulted roof. Around the patio are three buildings with rooms connected by narrow hallways. The last structure built at Mesa Verde is the Long House, so named because its 150 rooms extend over 300 feet (90 meters). In these photos are several kivas—circular structures dedicated to the ritual ceremonies of the Anasazi community.

Life on the Great Plains centered around the hunting of bison, or buffalo. The Indians used these game animals for everything, from building their homes to making clothing and shoes. They also ate them.

The Great Plains Indians led a nomadic life. They lived in seasonal camps, and their homes were the typical Indian tents: tepees made by covering wooden poles with bison hides. The life of the people was tied to the movements of the animals. They moved from camp to camp, following the migrating buffalo herds.

The cultivation of tobacco was widespread among these Indians. They raised it at their summer campgrounds.

The Woodland Cultures

A number of prehistoric cultures thrived in the northeastern woodlands of what is now the United States. At first they chiefly raised grains, squash, tobacco, and corn. Two interesting groups living in that area were the Adena and Hopewell peoples. They thrived from around 200 B.C. to A.D. 500. One of their outstanding achievements was their construction of great funeral mounds. These were structures used for burial, completed in wood and surrounded by earthen ramps. The Adena and Hopewell cultures became highly developed and used copper and silver. They decorated their pottery with reliefs and engravings.

Bison Cliff

At the end of the Pleistocene era, the glaciers melted. The northern forests gradually retreated and were eventually replaced by plains. These plains were a perfect setting for large herds of herbivores, or plant-eating animals. The rolling, grassy plains provided endless stretches of grazing land. Bison populations are estimated to have numbered in the millions. The bison became the material and spiritual center of life on the Great Plains.

Life on this land, which covers some 770,000 square miles (2 million square kilometers), was very hard for the early natives in many ways. But the Indians were excellent hunters. They used stealth, their knowledge of bison behavior, and their stone-tipped spears to hunt their prey.

Pastures as Bait
In southwestern Alberta, Canada, Bison Cliff is one of the most spectacular of the hunting sites known as bison jumps. The site has three distinct zones: the gathering valley, the field of slaughter, and the butchering area. In the top photo, with the Livingston Range in the background, is the basin of Olsen Creek. With over 12 square miles (32 square kilometers) of grazing land, it was a perfect place for gathering the bison herds, which were later driven toward the cliff.

One hunting method they used was the bison jump. They pursued the bison herds, ambushed them, and drove them toward steep cliffs. Pushed forward by the Indians and by the rest of the herd, the bison plunged to their death. Ten thousand years ago, Indians used this technique to kill anywhere from a few bison to hundreds. A historic tribe called the Blackfeet was one of the groups that used the method. In fact, many plains tribes along the eastern slope of the Rocky Mountains, from Canada to southern Colorado, used the bison jump technique.

Today, a site called Bison Cliff is being protected. It is located in southeastern Alberta, Canada. Three distinct areas can be seen at the cliff site: the gathering valley, the field of slaughter, and the butchering area.

The gathering valley, where the bison were led before going over the cliff, is a great prairie in the basin of Olsen Creek. From here, members of the tribe directed the herd along a route marked by heaps of stone, or cairns. Along the way, hunters lay hidden behind the cairns.

The Butchering Area

The cliff from which the bison were driven to their death is 60 feet (18 meters) high. In the past it was over 100 feet (30 meters) high. This change in height was caused by a growing deposit at the base of the cliff. It was formed by bison bones, manure, hides, butchering utensils, and the remains of other animals. Even some human remains were buried there. And there were centuries of wind-blown dust. In some places this deposit is 36 feet (11 meters) thick. Its oldest layers date back 5,700 years.

The Fountain of Eternal Youth

When did the Spaniards first set foot on North American soil? What sent them there? Their interest in colonizing new territory was heightened by myths and fables about the new land. This was the case for Juan Ponce de Leon. Almost by accident, he arrived in Florida as he searched for the fountain of eternal youth. The tale of the fountain combined classical myth with native American traditions of the New World. The miraculous waters were believed to turn old people into youths. The fountain was thought to be in the Bahamas' Bimini Islands, which had been discovered but not officially explored.

According to the myth, Bimini was an earthly paradise, where people lived without wars or confrontations and were always happy. They never grew old, thanks to the waters of their magic fountain. When King Ferdinand of Spain heard the story, he ordered Ponce de Leon (first governor of Puerto Rico) to head an exploring expedition.

With this official mandate, Ponce de Leon left Puerto Rico in 1512. He arrived in Florida the following year. He named it "Florida" because he arrived on Easter Sunday—Pascua Florida ("Festival of Flowers").

But Ponce de Leon did not discover the famous fountain. After exploring Florida, he realized it was not an island at all, but a peninsula inhabited by unfriendly Indians.

At a given moment, the Indians sprang out from their hiding places, screaming and frightening the herd. The startled animals raced toward the cliff and plunged into the abyss. At Bison Cliff today are found deposits of bone 36 feet (11 meters) thick in some places. The deepest layers are about 5,700 years old.

After killing the last wounded animals, the hunters began their main work: flaying the meat, removing the viscera, and cutting each animal into pieces small enough to be carried.

The hides, the meat, and some of the bones were then taken to the butchering area. There the meat was cut into strips to be dried in the sun. The hides were prepared for tanning, a process that turns raw hides into leather. The whole tribe worked together, including the women and children.

In more recent times, the bison became a sacred figure among these civilizations. The Sun Dance, celebrated during the bison's breeding season, was one of the greatest religious events of the year. Among the Blackfeet Indians of the northern Rocky Mountain region, the leader of the hunt was one of the most powerful members of the tribe. On him depended the prestige and wealth of the community.

Anthony Island

Off the coast of Canada's British Columbia lies a group of islands known as the Queen Charlotte Islands. One of these islands is only a tiny dot of land, but it is very interesting to archaeologists: Anthony Island.

Although Anthony Island is uninhabited today, the Haida Indians lived there for some two thousand years. These native people fished the rivers and coastal waters from canoes, each made from a single cedar trunk. Only a few traces remain of this civilization. These include two caves with burial remains; four campsites where community activities took place; and the ruins of Ninstints, or "the Town of the Red Codfish." In this village stand the Haida civilization's oldest cedar totem poles.

The village of Ninstints is located in the middle of Anthony Island. There can be seen the remains of ancient Haida dwellings, all constructed of cedar planks. Before them stand totem poles carved with each family's ancestral emblems.

The life of the Haida people was intimately tied to the western red cedar tree. With its wood, they made practically everything they used in everyday life.

Ancient Totem Poles
Unfortunately, the totem poles and burial sites of Anthony Island are in poor condition. To build them, the Haida Indians used their best available material: the wood of the western red cedar. This wood was also used to make tools, canoes, and houses. The island's damp climate has caused the poles to deteriorate.

18

A Village of Fishermen

L'Anse aux Meadows Historic Site was occupied for five hundred years. Its inhabitants were Norsemen, or Vikings, who came from Greenland and Iceland. The eight buildings that still stand today have been largely restored. Fishing was the main occupation in this community. The settlement was discovered in 1960 by the Norwegian archaeologist Helge Ingstad. This photo shows one of the houses in the fishing village.

Some of the Haida Indians' cedar artifacts included houses, canoes, totem poles, coverings to protect them from the rain, headdresses, platters and bowls, and various tools and hand-carved figures. Due to the extremely damp climate, most of these artifacts are badly damaged. Without care, they will disintegrate completely.

Although they were active warriors against their neighbors, the Haida lived in harmony with their environment. They were organized into clans, each of which honored its own totem. A totem is a symbolic emblem, such as a certain animal, that represents a clan and its ancestors. Fishing was the main occupation. The species most highly valued for food was the salmon. Salmon were caught in the river with bag nets and dams. On the high seas they were caught with hooks, spears, and nets. Crustaceans, or shellfish, also were highly prized. The women gathered them, digging them from the sand on the beach.

L'Anse aux Meadows National Historic Park

About five hundred years before Christopher Columbus reached the New World, the Norsemen (or Vikings) had already arrived on the coast of North America.

By the middle of the ninth century, the Vikings had colonized Iceland, an island in the North Atlantic Ocean. From there they sailed west in search of new lands to settle.

Scandinavian Dwellings in Newfoundland
According to the Scandinavian sagas, Leif Eriksson, son of Erik the Red, sailed west from Greenland at the beginning of the eleventh century. He landed at a point on the Atlantic Ocean that may have been the northern coast of Newfoundland. Perhaps this is the place known today as L'Anse aux Meadows. Here we can see the remains of a workshop for repairing boats (*upper right*); a structure of wood and earth (*lower right*); and a general view of the settlement (*left*).

The stories of these events are related in the sagas—written collections of Norse history and legends. According to the sagas, one of these Vikings, Erik the Red, was exiled from Iceland for murder. He decided to head out to sea and explore unknown shores. What he discovered was a bleak, windswept island, which he named Greenland. Leif Eriksson, his son, inherited his adventurous spirit. He set sail westward across the ocean and discovered an island where vines and wheat grew. He called this place Vinland, or "Land of Wine."

Eriksson decided to spend the winter there, and his men built a small village. They called it *Leifsbudir,* meaning the "House of Leif." When spring came, they returned to Greenland. When they arrived, Leif Eriksson described the marvels of the newly discovered land and organized a colonizing expedition. But when the Vikings got back to their New World settlement, they discovered they were not the only people there. They had to deal with the natives, whom they called *skraelingar,* meaning "cowards."

There has been much discussion about the exact location of Leif's settlement. It appears that it was at the northernmost tip of the Canadian island of Newfoundland.

In 1960, a Norwegian archaeologist, Helge Ingstad, discovered L'Anse aux Meadows, a Norse settlement at the northern tip of Newfoundland. At the site he found the foundations of eight typically Norse constructions.

Pre-Columbian Structures
On the eve of Christopher Columbus's arrival in the New World, there were about forty million inhabitants in the Americas. The arrival of Europeans brought about a major decline in the native population. Many civilizations completely disappeared. These photos show two distinct types of dwellings: those of the Viking style in L'Anse aux Meadows *(top)* and the structures built into the rocky cliffs at Mesa Verde *(bottom).*

Special Terms

beating for game: Frightening animals and chasing them to a predetermined place.

Inuit: Name by which the Canadian Eskimos refer to themselves. It means "the people" or "the true people."

kayak: One-person boat used by the Eskimos. It has a narrow hull, covered tightly with seal skins, and an opening in the middle where the rider sits with legs stretched out straight.

Pleistocene: Glacial era, one of the most important geological periods, lasting almost two million years.

saga: Epic tale that relates the heroic and mythological traditions of Scandinavians, including the Norsemen.

umiak: Eskimo boat larger than the kayak, with a seal skin cover stretched over a wood frame. It is used for hunting in a group, as in whale-hunting.

All of these buildings were used as dwellings or as workshops. The archaeologists assigned each building a letter to identify it. The largest is F, which, judging from its size, may have been Leif's quarters.

Mesa Verde National Park

Mesa Verde National Park is located in southwestern Colorado. Here the Anasazi Indians settled some 1,300 years ago. They were to become one of the best-known and most highly developed prehistoric cultures in North America.

Archaeologists call the first inhabitants of Mesa Verde the Basketmakers. These people lived in houses that were partially dug into the ground. Their descendants began to construct elevated buildings of wood and clay, with connected rooms. These buildings surrounded the kiva, an underground ceremonial chamber. In around the twelfth century, they began to build stone houses that were several stories high.

At the Mercy of the Weather
Its location and its altitude—from 6,000 to 8,600 feet (1,830 to 2,620 meters)—give Mesa Verde a harsh, rugged climate. Summers are very hot, and the winters are very cold with heavy snowfall. This gives us an idea of the hardships that the Anasazi must have suffered as they carved their cities out of the cliffs in such a hostile climate.

Cahokia Mounds

More than 120 mounds once existed at Cahokia Mounds. All of them were built for specific purposes. There were the platform or double platform mounds, upon which wooden buildings were erected. There were cone-shaped mounds, which were probably used for burials. And there were ridge-topped mounds—possibly for burials, but also used to observe astronomical alignments. All were built in a very organized way and show careful workmanship. This photo shows a typical mound, which the Cahokians built near a lake.

The people of Mesa Verde also constructed "cliff dwellings." These homes on sheer cliff faces were also several stories high, but fixed to the cliffs and cut from the rock. The ruins that remain show that this was one of the most beautiful cities in pre-Hispanic America. Outstanding among its buildings is Balcony House. It consists of a large interior patio with a vaulted ceiling. This is surrounded by three buildings, their rooms connected by narrow hallways. The Long House, dating from the second half of the thirteenth century, appears to be the last one built. Along the canyon walls extend 150 rooms covering some 300 feet (90 meters). This city is also notable for its twenty-one kivas.

Cahokia Mounds Historic Site

In southern Illinois, near the confluence of the Missouri and Mississippi rivers stand the remains of Cahokia. There lived one of North America's most important pre-Columbian cultures: the Mississippian culture.

Archaeologists have found nearly one hundred mounds there. These mounds provide a perfect opportunity to study the life of North America's pre-Columbian tribes. The name Cahokia is derived from the tribes that lived there when French explorers first arrived in the area.

Though fewer than thirty mounds remain in good condition, it is known that nearly all of them were built for specific purposes. There are platform mounds, or mounds with double platforms, where wooden buildings were erected; cone-shaped mounds, apparently used for burials; and ridge-topped mounds, possibly built for the same purpose but also used to observe astronomical alignments.

The main construction is Monk's Mound. This may have been the political and ceremonial center of the city. It is some 985 feet (300 meters) long, 660 feet (200 meters) wide, and 100 feet (30 meters) high. This is the largest mound north of the Valley of Mexico.

Burial remains found in Mound 72 reflect some of the customs of the Mississippian people. Members of the ruling class were buried among rich furnishings. The remains of more than three hundred people have been found here. Some were from the ruling elite, while others were sacrificed victims.

On the edge of the Cahokia Mound site, archaeologists have found traces of astronomical observatory. The Indians used it to calculate the annual cycle of the sun.

Traces of Indian Tribes
Hundreds of tribes inhabited North America at the time Columbus arrived. Many have survived and are undergoing a cultural revival today. Evidence of the early cultures still exist, such as the totem poles of Anthony Island; the massive earthworks of Cahokia Mounds; the cliff dwellings of Mesa Verde; the earthen houses of L'Anse aux Meadows; and the deposits of bones at Bison .Cliff. UNESCO has declared all of these places to be World Heritage sites.

30

These Sites Are Part of the World Heritage

Bison Cliff (Canada): In southwestern Alberta, Bison Cliff is spectacular testimony of one of the oldest hunting methods of the human species: bison jumps.

Anthony Island (Canada): This tiny island, part of the Queen Charlotte Archipelago, is the best example of pre-Columbian totem pole construction. The Haida Indians lived here for thousands of years, their lives intimately tied to salmon, western red cedar, and other plants and animals in the environment.

L'Anse aux Meadows National Historic Park (Canada): Discovered in 1960 by a Norwegian archaeologist, L'Anse aux Meadows is the definitive proof that a Viking settlement existed at the northernmost point of Newfoundland, centuries before Columbus reached the New World.

Mesa Verde National Park (United States): Mesa Verde National Park is located in southwestern Colorado. Here, about 1,300 years ago, the Anasazi Indians established one of the best-known and most highly developed prehistoric cultures in North America.

Cahokia Mounds Historic Site (United States): In southern Illinois, near the confluence of the Missouri and Mississippi rivers, are the remains of the mounds that comprised the center of Mississippian culture. For this reason, Cahokia is an archaeological center for learning about North America's pre-Columbian cultures of the Mississippi River Valley.

Glossary

adobe: a building material made of sun-dried mud mixed with straw

Amerindians: native peoples of the Americas

archaeologist: a scientist who studies the remains of human life in the past

archipelago: a group of islands

astronomical: having to do with stars, planets, and other heavenly bodies

cairn: a piled-up heap of stones

confluence: a flowing together or joining

deteriorate: to fall into worse condition or fall apart

elite: a group of people with high social class

epidemic: an outbreak of a disease that spreads throughout a community

fjord: a narrow inlet of water with steep cliffs along its edges

flay: to strip off the skin or surface

glacier: a great block of ice that moves down a mountainside or through a valley

mandate: an order or an approval to do something

motif: a repeated design, idea, or theme in a piece of art

nomadic: not settled; moving one's residence from place to place

prestige: status or importance

relief: a sculptured surface that stands out from the background

sedentary: settled down; living in one place

stealth: secrecy or sneakiness

sub-Arctic: region just south of the Arctic Circle

tundra: in cold regions, a plain with frozen subsoil and no trees

vaulted: arched; curved

viscera: internal organs of the body

Index

Page numbers in boldface type indicate illustrations.

Titles in the World Heritage Series

The Land of the Pharaohs
The Chinese Empire
Ancient Greece
Prehistoric Rock Art
The Roman Empire
Mayan Civilization
Tropical Rain Forests of Central America
Inca Civilization
Prehistoric Stone Monuments
Romanesque Art and Architecture
Great Animal Refuges
Coral Reefs
Australia: Land of Natural Wonders
Pre-Columbian Peoples of North America
The Mughal Empire
The Empire of the Czars

Photo Credits

Front Cover: E. Anderson/Incafo; p. 5: L. Alonso & M. G. Fernandez/Incafo; p. 7: E. Anderson/Incafo; p. 9: E. Anderson/Incafo; p. 11: A. Larramendi/Incafo; p. 13: A. Larramendi/Incafo; p. 15: E. Anderson; p. 17: E. Anderson/Incafo; p. 19: E. Anderson/Incafo; p. 21: E. Anderson/Incafo; p. 22: E. Anderson/Incafo; p. 23: E. Anderson/Incafo; p. 25: E. Anderson/Incafo; A. Larramendi/Incafo; p. 26: A. Larramendi/Incafo; pp. 27, 29: L. Alonso & M. G. Fernandez/Incafo; p. 31: E. Anderson/Incafo; L. Alonso & M. G. Fernandez/Incafo; A. Larramendi/Incafo; E. Anderson/Incafo; back cover: E. Anderson/Incafo; A. Larramendi/Incafo.

Project Editor, Childrens Press: Ann Heinrichs
Original Text: Maria Cordoba
Subject Consultant: Dr. Robert B. Pickering
Translator: Deborah Kent
Design: Alberto Caffaratto
Cartography: Modesto Arregui
Phototypesetting: Publishers Typesetters Inc.

UNESCO's World Heritage

The United Nations Educational, Scientific, and Cultural Organization (UNESCO) was founded in 1946. Its purpose is to contribute to world peace by promoting cooperation among nations through education, science, and culture. UNESCO believes that such cooperation leads to universal respect for justice, for the rule of law, and for the basic human rights of all people.

UNESCO's many activities include, for example, combatting illiteracy, developing water resources, educating people on the environment, and promoting human rights.

In 1972, UNESCO established its World Heritage Convention. With members from over 100 nations, this international body works to protect cultural and natural wonders throughout the world. These include significant monuments, archaeological sites, geological formations, and natural landscapes. Such treasures, the Convention believes, are part of a World Heritage that belongs to all people. Thus, their preservation is important to us all.

Specialists on the World Heritage Committee have targeted over 300 sites for preservation. Through technical and financial aid, the international community restores, protects, and preserves these sites for future generations.

Volumes in the *World Heritage* series feature spectacular color photographs of various World Heritage sites and explain their historical, cultural, and scientific importance.